slowly
but
surely

growth is still growth.

slowly but surely

APARNA RAY

ARCHWAY
PUBLISHING

Archway Publishing books may be ordered
through booksellers or by contacting:

Archway Publishing
1663 Liberty Drive
Bloomington, IN 47403
www.archwaypublishing.com
844-669-3957

Because of the dynamic nature of the Internet, any web
addresses or links contained in this book may have changed
since publication and may no longer be valid. The views
expressed in this work are solely those of the author and do
not necessarily reflect the views of the publisher, and the
publisher hereby disclaims any responsibility for them.

Any people depicted in stock imagery provided by Getty Images are
models, and such images are being used for illustrative purposes only.
Certain stock imagery © Getty Images.

ISBN: 978-1-6657-1543-0 (sc)
ISBN: 978-1-6657-1542-3 (hc)
ISBN: 978-1-6657-1544-7 (e)

Library of Congress Control Number: 2021923725

Print information available on the last page.

Archway Publishing rev. date: 3/4/2022

To my Aii, you are my whole world. Not a moment
passes that I do not think of you. Words and time are
the greatest gift you gave me and for that I am forever
grateful. I owe you my life, love and language. And
finally to my mother. My life's blood and my
greatest strength. Each victory belongs to
us together as one. This book is for you.

i want you to paint through my veins
and fill them with all the wishes that were never fulfilled.
so that each step i take
will be breathing proof
of my dedication
to dreams.

never let go
because your hands
feel like home.

it was a good kind of cry though.
the kind you need to feel.
the kind that makes you feel alive and alone.
all at once,
in seven shades of blue.

you remind me of
the stars on my ceiling.
silent and bright.
something everyone sees,
but not everyone looks for.
loud with no words.
firmly settled in yourself.

you are not made to fit.
but no one ever tells you that.
some are not meant to fall into place.
some must fight.
some must claw.
some must fall.
but you and me?
we must search.
and i have walked my journey.
climbed walls
and scaled mountains.
and i'm so happy to have found you.
waiting at the end.
for me.

i am drawn.
i am painted.
but i will never be contained on canvas.

do you ever think,
life moves,
just a little slower,
for some people?

why do i love you?
i have asked myself
every single day
since the day we met.
you stuck with me.
that's why.
no matter how hard i tried to forget.
you stayed.
i didn't say a word.
we continued along our paths.
of meaningless kisses
and tired hands.
//
but now,
you swing for another.
you write for another.
you feel. for another.
and now, i refuse.
i refuse to remain silent.
i will say a word.
i will say as many as i want.
as many as it takes.
as many to make you realize.
how you are,
inexplicably made for me.

yes.
i admit.
it scares me.
it frightens me.
our last words.
our last kiss.
will not be enough.
i will be forgotten so quickly.
while i love you
more by dawn.

I wanted to inhabit these feelings,
and give their demise
a meaning.

i'm very forgettable.
there's nothing special about me
i come and i go.
no one misses the way i kiss
or how I speak.
i'm just a faint memory.
something in between.
a temporary fix.

a little part of me,
thinks i always did.
i didn't know how to say it.
or even how to feel it.
but i knew it.
we both did.
i always did love you.

sweet lime and jacky,
physically apart,
but always in one another's hearts.
i find it odd,
that we found one another
long ago,
but only saw each other
yesterday,
and yet,
when we are together now,
i feel like i don't have to miss you.
as if i have been longing for you,
all these years.
i feel so
complete. and finished.

love is,
saying yes,
when you cannot say no,
saying why,
just to hear them speak,
and saying i love you,
when you know they know,
but you say it anyway.

i am so content
with the idea
and reality
of us.

kiss my cheeks
with cherry lips
and tulips.

but you did not repair,
you swept me under her rug,
and hoped to forget.

unrelenting love,
we whispered sweet convictions,
through holes no one else saw.

the eighth world wonder,
when our love ran rampant,
through the muddy streets
of hell.

one day i forgot.
i forgot to be sad,
and fall at your dear feet.
that was the day.
oh that was it.
the day i buried your memories
in the same grave,
my love lied years ago.

my name is spoken with such reverence.
and with that,
i claw my way into the mouths of many.
but when it slips from your lips,
my jaw locks,
my knees buckle,
and once again,
i am at the mercy
of your tender words,
and fierce game

we used pen.
marking the future
we set in stone
and watched it tumble.

and fellow lovers
fell at your feet.
yesterday,
today,
and tomorrow,
to ask,
for the rest of your life.

when i was a child,
i used to think heartburn
was when you had love for someone,
with warm words and the hands of an angel.
and they crushed you.
with their lack of love.
and made your heart ache.

somehow your hollow words,
and crass voice comforted
the red pen
that had been written
through my eyes
and
between my fingertips.

my mother once said
i cry with empty eyes
an open heart
and bowed hands

sometimes when i
wake up scared at night,
i am comforted,
by the stars
i put up long ago.
and i dream
i live far far away

we run and hide.
scared of the demons
we see.
it makes us weary.
for we cannot
escape the demons
that awaken
within us.

it's scary to think
that i'm always so close
so close to that cliff,
waiting.
upon that edge.

now when i do,
by the time i begin,
i am already finished.

do we hide behind
these masks
because we are afraid of what they think
or because we
are terrified of how
small we are.
how little we matter?
//
once again i ask you,
do we hide behind
these masks,
because we are afraid
of what they will see?
or because we are scared
of what we will show?
//
one last time i ask you,
do we hide behind
these masks,
because we are afraid
of what we will see?
or because we are scared
of what they will show?

intents snugly
blanketed by
blatant remarks
and callous rewards.

today i reject.
today i reject it all.
i devote myself,
to pure and simple hedonism,
and devout i will be.

who are you to say so?
have you found so much grief?
so much grief at the bottom of your silver chalice?
or perhaps skirting your plate?
no.
for you fall short in one thing.
you did not watch your life
tossed into remorseless destruction,
as we did.
that is where you are found,
a lacking.

i will bloom.
with such darkling deviance
and remain unscathed
due to your infallible efforts
to cure me with gold.
despite the copper tones
i regret to reflect.

as delicately as you
say my name.
with daises cut
neatly along my edges.

i hope that one day
i hold you.
i hope that one single day,
i hold you,
in the palm of my hand,
intertwined with
my champagne-colored words,
and fickle intentions.

we are crippling.
crippling in grief.
holding on still,
to the hell
in which we met our ends.

we are tangled
in one another
somewhere
in between
together.

dull sober tugs
seek to arise me
seeping through
soft cracks
and bitter tusks.
i simply wonder,
how such a flimsy veil
has held its own for centuries.
and had no trouble
herding the masses
and parading the tacks.

i used to defy affections
that came with ease,
thinking that anything
so simple,
could never be so sweet.
but your manifestation of love,
so copious,
so pure,
and thus i accepted,
love.
the way it should be.
with acquiesce.

we lie so still
so far.
and laced
in our sweet cocoon
of infatuation.

one day.
i hope you will confess.
about how you fell.
how you fell in love,
with the way i dance,
and the way i trace your skin.

our hearts may not
beat to the same rhythm anymore,
but i will continue.
bearing testament
to your sporadic and ardent affection.

you speak with
such grace and sentiment,
i nearly forget,
how the words
sting.

empty eyes.
and callous hands.
brush the hair from my face.
and pain from my lips.

tender glances
and shallow words,
seek to tug my heartstrings.
pull the pain
you forgot was there.

soft faceless creations
to numb the fallen tips
of those who forgot us.

cross borne
between your lips
you are mine.
sacrilegious beast.

but every second
i stay there,
i feel a small part of me,
crumble away.
i feel a small part of me,
die a little bit,
each and every day.

hold my hand.
one last time
and pretend.
pretend you love me.
pretend i am her.

we wish upon stars.
eyes shut so tight
praying for something
miraculous to happen.
because we are so tired
of feeling so very
hopeless.
torn.

i hope one day,
regardless of whether i see it,
or not
you find your twinkle again.
the twinkle
that melted my heart
and buckled my knees.
you lost it in years past,
and i admit,
i did not aid you in the search.
i allowed it to get lost.
in the raging sea of her love.

you fluster me
with such charm and ease
that i fall.
i fall victim.
once again,
i fall victim,
to your tender colloquy.

we spoke of things
we knew not.
things we called love.
but we spoke with one another
with such ardency
and ferver,
that our honeyed lips,
and cherubic nuances believed.
believed every word we spilled.
coaxingly.
falling
deeper into one another.

somehow,
my name sounds just
a little more mellifluous.
oh how i long
how i long for your sweet melodies
to sing me to sleep

just one night
to fall in love.
with the way you speak,
and the manner in which
you say my name.
just one night.
all over again.

enter.
into the swelling river
to find sounds.
so dry,
the cuts speak.

but i am unapologetic
do not forgive my loud thoughts.
ask why,
why you felt so threatened,
by my rousing words,
and nuanced ideas.

unable to fly away
caught in your nest
unable to sting myself.

swaying in your sea,
i will always remain
a reclusive lover.

breathe me in,
like a promise,
breaking,
the moment we kissed sweet words.

my heart grew tipsy
with affections
steeped in lies
about how our love
was forever.
running out of time
trying to show you
that you,
already won.

it laced the wings of doves
falling from the pale skies
and bitter clouds.

the kind of person
who has something to say.
you do not waste words.
so kindly my love,
indulge me,
and speak.

my dear,
our love is forsaken,
how did you leave so long
tomorrow?

clenched teeth
and clasped hands
to beg for salvation,
to fall upon
and sacred words
to take touch.

for the world is in mourning,
it observes as your sweet lips
slip through.

paint through
the cracked walls.
and meet me
in the middle.
with blank eyes
and sober lips,
our fingertips
meet and listen.

we promised.
we promised
never to look back
on our battered
and coaxed love.

fall in love
with the sound
of our voices
together.

even then,
maybe,
i'll sew my heart on your sleeve
so the world sees
how unbreakable
we remain.
I am so tired.
i am so tired of loving you
and forgetting,
to love myself.

they don't fall the same way anymore.
i've lost.
and i am so aware of that loss.
i hope one day you realize.
i'm looking at you
and have been.
and you may have forgotten me,
but no,
i have not forgotten you.

we flee.
to beds unmade,
and promises unkept
to hide from words unspoken
and holes unfilled.

please never come,
if you ever leave.
lack,
not loss.
let go.
let me.

today is the day
i can recall tomorrow
as if yesterday.

let your walls down.
wipe my soul
on your welcome mat.
and greet me,
with open arms
and loving lips.

i love to watch you
prance about,
behind the walls
you built high enough
to protect yourself
from people
who never hurt you.

oh but you do not understand,
the storm does not begin when we speak.
it begins when we break to breathe.
it is when all our confrontations cease.
and we halt.
we no longer fight.
for each other.

the only thing
i hate more
than you waking me up
is waking up
without you.

please never forget
that the only hand
you should dream of holding,
is your own.

push back the waves
and envelope me
with sweet words,
tainted
with sea salt.

why we stood with pride
and they congregated
as if we would fall.
as if we could fall.

sweet dulcet tones
oh why your voice comforted me
with its slow
warm rhythm
"oh sweet love of mine"
"i want someone to want me"
"too much love to give"

oh he loved me less
my days stood slow
and still
he loved me longer

fingertips danced through
your love keeps me up at night
i let myself down

he said he writes poetry.
he said he writes poetry,
about the way i look,
when i speak.

fall as you might,
i will still see
the great stories you lived
and the beasts you slayed.

dancing in the window pane
waiting for the sun
to play along with me

i believed we fell,
at the same moment,
on opposite ends
into the same lagoon,
of fleeting love,
and everlasting games.
unfortunately now,
i realize,
that you jumped,
and i tripped.
and that is why,
we will never find salvation,
in one another.

when will we find it?
if we continue to search
within those
who fall behind
and those
who simply spill ahead.

a sweet kind of sad
like honey laced in venom
and roses pricked on thorns.
a sad kind of sweet
like the twinkle in your tears
and dust on your words.

but no
i don't love you
any longer.
you forgot me
and i lay your thoughts
to rest.

decades
we wait
for winds that never blow
and storms that never come.
that is why we fell
we fell into each other
by accident.
never with purpose.
always lacking intent.

your fingers
laced through mine
and reminded me
of the way
he used to hold me

brotherhood befalls you
as my dear sweet carnations
lay them to rest

my momentary lapse
has proven weary
perusing all
the forgotten words
and worn out dances.

god how i wish.
how i wish
you would look at me
even if it be
with pain and regret
to see your blossoming eyes,
would be the most wretched gift
i've ever wanted to collect.

all at once
seized the pain and pleasure
took me
so desolate and void.
stumble through
the coarse words
to find you.
waiting.
with open arms
ready,
ready to crash and burn.
together at last.

i am sorry to say
i must leave sir
i loved to play
but i am not her.

somber tones
to ease your toffee colored rinds
and soothe your pious mouth

why is it
that when i come out
the sun feels
so dusty
so stale
as if falling.

in a crowded room
i slip away searching,
yes,
searching,
for your face.

you hold my hand
with such vigor
and tenacity,
i forget
that you want her.

i carried you through
breaking myself
bleeding black
to watch you fall
into her arms.

why do i watch
as i break myself
to put you
back together

i am so very tired.
so very tired
of feeling lifeless,
like an empty shell,
of who i used to be.

we wrote our lives out
on the same scrap of paper
so why am i the only one
scrambling
to save it.

i tripped i fell
through the wall
i saw you
in the hole
oh how you made me pale
oh how you made me whole.

we met
in a time
of great loss
of greed.
i found my ends in,
in the chains,
the chains
you freed.
yes,
i guess i did
lose my heart,
but not to you.
i kept your heart
in my pocket
tucked away
safe
from the raging sea
why did you steal mine
and feed it
to your honey (bee)

clutching real
just a little tighter
holding it
between my fingers
begging for it
to just
let
go.

the thoughts flooded me
but only when we were apart.
when we separated,
my heart spoke
and sulked,
when we united,
your expressions
crouched over my lines
and blew me away.
the slit in your voice.
and snake in your words.
and somehow,
i grew to love.
i grew to love the pain.

the light in the corner,
glows brighter when it is dark.
you too, glow brighter.

do not adjust your name
so that
it fits in their mouths
do not adjust your words
so that
they rest untouched
do not adjust your voice
so that
it does not get silenced

it was never me.
the kisses on the cheek
the way you looked in my eyes
you saw her.
and that is all i'll ever get to be.

sometimes i wish.
i wished i fit the mold.
i wished each glance,
would be spoken about
with great reverence.
mostly i wished for you.
but we all know,
wishes,
rarely come true.

i watch
as they slip away,
soft through my fingertips.
i run
chasing them
reaching to the sky.
i stop
catching my breath,
losing my life.

i crawl
in the shadows
hiding around
each corner
hoping
praying
i do not find
my surprise

each breath
holds a lifetime
each dream
regret and touch
rest peacefully,
unbothered by the shadows
cast through selfish windows,
locked away
with all the words
left unsaid.

my sweet hummingbird,
the serenity of your voice
flows through
seeking out,
my gentle hands.

the grasp of
your words
holds me
close.

like the birds in the wind,
they soar.
watching
and breathing in
all of you.
just you.

just out of reach.
so close to grasp.
so sweet to touch.
so hard to hold.
toes curled
and weapons drawn.
i left to find.
to find someone who believed.
who believed i was
so soft to hold.
so warm to feel.
so gentle to slip.
so content to be.

it has begun to sour
the words that meander
across your lips.
you grew restless
tired of the long
lessons and
tedious lives

so tender and delicate.
so sweet and precise.
your words are as effortless,
as they are intentional.

i told myself never again.
after the pain and sorrow.
the hurt and healing.
but here we are again.
turning around.
only to slip and fall.
or was it skip and float.
into your arms.
and that's when i remembered,
why i said no before.
your arms were not open.
i missed.

the twinkle in your eyes
i watched the love fall away
the waltz in your words
we never said bye
i forgot to forget you
and now i dance on my own.

soulful leaps soared on
somehow your hands remembered
minds,
in all their glory

your hands screamed my name
and eyes shouted with might
all your tacit love

but i will not yield
you pinky swore never to forgot
my soft skin
and pink lips

you are a new kind of person.
a kind the world has never seen before.
the culture of you,
is a superlative in itself.
you demand attention.

they say grow
they explain push
but their hopeful
does not align
my realistic

my voice is a wave
devouring all that
stand in the way.
it consumes the greats
and dresses the weak.
they crave it
knowing full well
it will leave them
wanting more
every
time.

my words.
run parallel to velvet
plush push pins
pierce each paragraph
that spill from my
lips and drip
from my fingertips.
you know you wish.
wish i would continue
but i know.
that is all that keeps
you coming back.

the sweet release
beckons me,
taunting me with
rest and peace.
i fight for you.
the pain processes
outside of my being
when i see.
when i see your tears.
when i see your hurt.
and i mask my own
in order to pull
those tears
back to the paradise
they hinder.

your fingers
used to taste like tea.
nowadays
they taste like me.

all people want
is sovereignty.
all people
need is perspective.

only halfway here
hoping to
help your hurt
healing my heart

loving you
feels like
collecting colors
each moment so different
and so cherished.
each shade
held so close.

the day we met
i found my clover.
i kept it close.
scared of
losing the luck
i never had
in the first place.

this glass castle
was built to tumble.
it welcomed visitors
that were well aware.
well aware of its fate.
well aware of their fate.
well aware of our fate.

this springtime stroll
welcomes.
welcomes the swing time.
pushing through the pull
of simply
letting
go.

when the doves cry.
i will return.
to my final,
to my final resting place.
till then,
i am yours.

you should never
have to question love.
you should be
carrying the color of their eyes.
resting on their words.
dreaming in their hands.

i will love
your hands
for the both
of us.
till you can learn
to love them
for yourself.

she will.
she will blossom.
she will sip the wind and dance
        with me.
she will.
she will blossom.
she will carry the world and sing with the gods that
        don't see.
she will.
she will blossom.
she will blossom with or without
        a bee.

the frame of a new father
haunts me.
his words so hopeful.
my words so humbled.

sometimes,
i feel like paper,
trying to stretch.
stretch without tearing.
without tearing up.
yet somehow,
despite my best efforts,
the tears manage
manage to stream down
those cheeks
you once adored.

I was half dead
hoping to heal.
hoping to heal
the hurt you helped.

you remind me
of the daffodils
that bloom in the snow.
so hopelessly optimistic.
something i so admire.

your voice,
so warm and gentle,
guides me.
somewhere east of the sun.
rising and falling
in a manner
only understood by
you and me.

the clouds.
the clouds of smoke and thought
crowded the room.
you cut through it,
to rescue me from myself.

he said he loves my stretch marks.
they remind him
of the journeys we traveled
and lights turned dark.
morning felt long
and night fell fast.
your hands drifted
and met my hips
as if returning at last.
the comfort of your lips
taste like honey
slips like stone
and finally,
drops.

my bed is big enough for two
but my love, as much as it hurts,
it will never have room for you.

simple love
is very difficult to find
indeed it is
but the greatest challenge
is not finding it.
it is keeping it
for this world is unkind
nothing stays simple.

i prefer to listen.
although i hear myself speak.
i prefer to observe.
although i walk through the foreground.
i prefer to love and be loved.
although i often feel neither.

i say i flew
even when you feel like rain
you smell like dew.

these lips that tease
they draw her too.
these hands that please
they saw her too.

those photographs are gone.
burned in a fire long ago.
the fire raged on.
but the memory remained.
and that fire aches too.

her pain is palpable.
she thinks i do not see.
she believes i cannot see.
she is convinced my pain
drowns me and allows me
to pull away from reality
where she lies waiting
for my pain to come forth.
-----
i did not see.
i could not see.
i was selfish and saw only
the hurt inflicted to me.
-----
i am grown now.
i see it all.
i wish for a sea of naivety
to pull me deep.
but i see her lying there.
and i comfort the pain
she once saw in me.

there are no photographs.
there is no art.
in fear of the fleeting,
I left it blank.
i worried so deeply
that all would be lost
lacking even a moment's notice.

---

but now,
this emptiness surrounding me
provides me with a new sense of hope.
hope that it will fill.
hope that I will fill.
hope that even if it all passes,
it welcomes a new beginning,
much better than the old ending.

---

so here i stand,
waiting for the new dawn.
a day much more promising than the last.
for i can leave the last,
far far in the past.
and grow to love
the new sun.

these expectations,
they bind you.
they strap you down,
and tell you to hold on for dear life.
for most of the time,
people lose their lives,
trying to fulfill them.
all the while,
forgetting to fulfill,
them.

it is not in spite of these scars
that we grow stronger,
it is because of these scars,
we grow stronger.

CPSIA information can be obtained
at www.ICGtesting.com
Printed in the USA
LVHW030841200422
716605LV00007B/444

9 781665 715430